Overcoming the Struggles of *Singleness*

ASHLEY RENAÉ BALDRIDGE

Ashley Renae' Baldridge
Purpose & Co. Ministries © 2016

Copyright © 2016 by Ashley R. Baldridge
ALL RIGHTS RESERVED

No part of this book may be reproduced, stored in a retrieval system, or transmitted in any form or by any means-electronic, mechanical, photocopy, recording, or otherwise-without prior written permission of the publisher, except for brief quotations used in connection with reviews in magazines or newspapers.

Cover design by Cre8ive Solutions
Interior design and formatting by House Capacity Publishing LLC
Unless otherwise specified, all Scripture quotations are taken from the Holy Bible

ISBN: 978-0-578-51201-3

This book is dedicated to my grandparents, Ida and William Reaves, Jr. I know you both would be proud of me. Granny, I'm doing all you said I would.
I'm getting my "EDU-MA-CATION!"
Love and miss you both dearly. You are forever in my heart.
To be absent from the body, is to be present with the Lord.

Contents

Acknowledgements	vii
Prayer	9
Trust	13
Friendship Over Loneliness	17
Opportunities Over Loneliness	21
Contentment, Not Envy	25
Patience	29
Hope Over Despair	33
Identity Crisis	37
Holiness, Not Sin	41
Guarding Your Heart	45
Blocking the Noise: Deceptive Voices	49
Overcoming Rejection	53
Breaking the Stronghold of Lust	57
Sure, Why Not? What Harm Could it Do?	61

Single and Loving it	65
See No Evil, Hear No Evil, Speak No Evil: Overcoming Temptations	69
Realize You Have Something to Offer	73
Forgiveness	77
What Glitters Isn't Gold: Relationship Goals	81
Fear: Reject Fearful Thoughts	85
Stop Criticizing Yourself	89
Can You Fix It? Yes, You Can!	93
God's Unconditional Love	97
Self-Discovery	101
Faith Over Fear	105
Comfortable with Yourself	109
Trust in the Lord: I Shall Remain Confident	113
A Blessing and a Curse	117

Acknowledgments

This book was inspired during Sunday morning worship. This particular Sunday, our guest speaker was Pastor Mary Bragg of Mount Moriah Christian Church. All I remember from that day is the moment I heard the Lord tell me to write a devotional for single women. From that moment, I sought God. Every word in this book was God-inspired and has been a blessing to me throughout this process.

I would first like to thank my Lord and Savior, Jesus Christ; without Him, none of this would have been possible; my parents, Levell and Regina Baldridge, who also double as my spiritual parents at New Birth Church of God in Christ; and to my sister, best friend, prayer partner and confidant, Tiffany Nichole`, I thank you and love you all. For your continued prayers and support and for speaking life into every situation that I have faced. Without my family and my support system, I wouldn't be the woman I am today.

I would like to also acknowledge Pastor DeAndre "D.R. Speaks" Riley for encouraging me to get it done, and Minister LaMonte Bird, my long-time friend, brother, and life coach, for his words of encouragement. I truly thank God for those who have followed me along this journey.

To Tenita "Bestseller" Johnson, I have called her the *midwife* of the writers. She pushes us daily with her social media posts, challenging authors or "authorpreneurs," to write that book, finish that book. To my sister, Shairon Taylor, thank you for praying, for your kind words and for even serving as editor of this book. To my spiritual father, Superintendent James A. Smith Jr., a man after God's heart. Growing up under your leadership made me who I am today. Because of your firm teaching, I am the bible scholar I am today. I will forever be grateful for the legacy that you have left with me.

My prayer is that lives will be impacted by this book.

A solemn request for help or expression of thanks addressed to God or an object of worship.
(Merriam-Webster Dictionary)

In the *War Room* devotional in the YouVersion mobile app, authors Alex and Stephen Kendricks discussed the following method of prayer entitled A.C.T.S. A.C.T.S. is an acronym for:

Adoration - *Praising, worshipping God for who He is*
Confession - *Asking God to cleanse us from sin*
Thanksgiving - *Believing, acknowledging God's grace*
Supplication - *Our specific prayer requests*

ACTS Method of Prayer

Adoration –The first and most important component of prayer is adoration. Beginning your prayer time with adoration is a powerful way to get focused on God. In this place of adoration, you're acknowledging God for all that He is to you. You're pushing self-serving requests out of mind, focusing solely on God and your relationship with Him. A few minutes of quiet meditation on God's Word or listening to short, exhorting sermons beforehand will tremendously help at this stage of prayer.

Confession – This is where we confess our sins, ask God for forgiveness and trust Him to cleanse us by the blood of Christ. We do this so that our prayers will not be hindered by sin. Psalms 139:23-24(KJV) say, *Search me, O God, and know my heart: try me, and know my thoughts: And see if there be any wicked way in me, and lead me in the way everlasting.* We ask for God to remove anything that is unlike Him, repent for things done knowingly or unknowingly. Psalms 51:10(KJV) says, *"Create in me a clean heart, O God: and renew a right spirit within me."* We must go before God with a clean heart.

Thanksgiving – This is where we give thanks to God for all things, acknowledging that all blessings come from God alone, along with believing and receiving these blessings. Always "glorify him with thanksgiving," Psalms 69:30(NIV). You have plenty of reasons to be thankful: for God's love towards us, His faithfulness, His patience and a million other things. Express gratitude for what He's doing in your life. Thank Jesus for dying on the cross for you. Thank the Holy Spirit for indwelling you and never leaving. Thank Him for being your conscience, your counselor and for that "still small voice."

Supplication - Now, you are ready to ask God for what you desire by making your requests known. You are now in a position to ask Him for all that you need, having the confidence that He will answer your prayer. "Make your requests known to God," Philippians 4:6(KJV)

Tell God what you want, no matter how big or small it may seem. You should have lots of intercessory prayer, making intercession for your pastor and your church daily.
(A.C.T.S. excerpts taken from *War Room Devotional,* YouVersion Bible App)

I'm a firm believer that prayer certainly changes things. Along with consecrating ourselves, we thrive off process and success. If prayers are conversations with God, consider your journaling like writing Him love notes. Writing allows you to look back on all the miracles and works He's performed in your life. It'll serve as a constant reminder that God can and God will perform that great work in your life. I encourage you to journal throughout this process—write out questions, things you identify with and use those as your prayer focus. At the end, you'll see a set of self-check questions. Allow these to be your prayer focus questions. As you journal, you will have a sense of what it is that you need to seek God for.

The following page is the template by which you may use to structure your prayer journal.

Daily Prayer

Praises

_____
_____
_____
_____
_____

Prayer Requests	Answered On

Trust

Trust is the firm belief in the reliability, truth, ability or strength of someone or something.
(Merriam-Webster Dictionary)

Many friendships and relationships start off at zero, with little to no in-depth knowledge about that person. This is the starting point of learning about the individual and growing to trust them. Once we've arrived at that place of being able to trust, a window of endless possibilities is opened. We begin to share little things about ourselves, even the things we may never share with anyone else. We must learn to monitor how we filter our deepest thoughts and secrets, while trusting in the one who will never leave or forsake us.

Where is your trust?

Trust in the Lord with all your heart and lean not on your understanding; in all your ways submit to him, and he will make your paths straight.
Proverbs 3:5-6 NIV

Oftentimes, we put all of our trust in man and forget about the One who made us and gave us life. We must trust in the One who yet is high and lifted up. We may have trusted others before and allowed them into our space. As a result, some take your kindness for weakness, oftentimes using those very secrets against you. Singles, we must guard our hearts and continue to trust in God's plan for our lives. Not everyone has a heart of gold; not everyone shares your values. We must stay focused on things that matter.

Prayer Affirmation

Father God, I ask that you touch us. Where we may no longer trust, I pray that you would build us up. Lord, restore our hearts to where we first met you, that we would trust you more than we trust anyone else. Lord I ask that you give us a heart of discernment. Lord, open our eyes so we may see people for who they really are and learn how to open up to others and to who

Amen.

Psalms 20:7, 31:14; John 14:1; Romans 15:13

Do you have trust issues?

1. Think of a few people who you trust. Do you trust these individuals with certain things or do they have all of your trust?
   _____
   _____

2. In what ways would you say you trust yourself?
   _____
   _____

3. How often does someone you trust betray you?
   _____
   _____

4. Do people have to earn your trust?
   _____
   _____

5. What, if any issues do you carry over from your past relationships?
   _____
   _____

6. When it comes to trust, what's your track record like? What is needed in order for you to trust an individual?
   _____
   _____

Friendship Over Loneliness

Friendship is a state of mutual trust and support between allied nations.
(Merriam-Webster Dictionary)

To properly establish friendships, we must first cultivate a relationship with the Father through Christ. Before we build our trust and hope in others, seek the one who has been there for you even when you didn't think anyone cared. If you've never had a real friend, I promise that you will wish you would've met Him sooner. Jesus is a friend who will never leave you. He'll never air your dirty laundry out for the entire world to see. The greatest friend you could ever have is in Jesus.

A man that hath friends must shew himself friendly: and there is a friend that sticketh closer than a brother.
Proverbs 18:24(KJV)

A relationship with Christ is one that follows you wherever you go. Cultivate your relationship with Him and watch how your outlook on friendships changes. By allowing God to love you wholeheartedly, He will show you what you've been missing. Oftentimes, we seek companionship, friends and intimate relationships to pacify the feelings of loneliness.

The reality is neither of those things will totally rid you of those feelings. While you may be happy for a moment, those feelings will creep back and before you know it, you'll be moving from one relationship to the next, which brings about inconsistency. Instead of looking for happiness in that new boyfriend, friends and family, all you have to do is look up.

Prayer Affirmation

Lord, please come into my life. I give you free reign and control in my life. Where I may be lonely, I ask that you fill the void. Come in like a flood and make me over again. Help me to make better decisions when it comes to choosing friends and companions. During this season of singleness, Lord, help me to grow in you, so I may become wiser and stronger. Open my eyes so I may see those who are for me and those who are not for me. Continue to go before me; show me the way in making right decisions. Amen.

Proverbs 12:26, 17:17; Ecclesiastes 4:9-10; John 15:12-15

Overcoming Loneliness

1. How do you feel when you're lonely?

_____
_____
_____
_____
_____
_____
_____

2. What do you do to stop the feeling? Is it possible? List the ways you can overcome and combat loneliness.

_____
_____
_____
_____
_____
_____
_____
_____

Opportunities Over Loneliness

A great friend of mine once told me, "instead of focusing on the difficulties, use the single state to serve God and His people." It's an opportunity to do things and go places that married people may not be able to go. When you're married, you must consult your husband before pursuing your next endeavor. Even Apostle Paul tells us to consult our spouses before fasting! (1 Corinthians 7:5)(KJV) If you have to consult your spouse concerning spiritual matters, what about the natural? You're no longer two but one. To keep your marriage flowing smoothly, you both must be on the same page. These are the things you must deal with in marriage. As a single, serving believer, you're only submitted to God. Therefore, be grateful for the freedom to come and go, operate in ministry and live your life.

While marriage looks good on the outside, there are always trials and situations that go down behind the scenes. We're in preparation mode during this time of singleness. This is the time where we ought to focus on ourselves, build our trust in God and cultivate our relationship with Christ. You can be a blessing by sharing your experiences with others who may have lost motivation or feel lonely.

This time of singleness has given me a lot of hope and inspiration. Instead of moping around feeling depressed, I have been creating new ideas, writing out my thoughts and executing them. I encourage you to utilize this time to birth new ideas, innovative concepts and do community outreach. Take this time to learn about yourself, how to apply your life experiences to something that would inspire and empower others.

Take Advantage of this Opportunity

Don't look at your singleness as a burden, and by all means, don't rush yourself into something you aren't totally ready for. You can jump into something prematurely and possibly ruin your chances of going further in the relationship. We must always seek God for direction and how to execute certain things. At some point in my dating life, I was the one who was always in control. I've recently met someone and I wanted that control. The mere fact that I couldn't make the calls or have things my way frustrated me. Ladies, if a man is genuinely interested in you, he will indeed pursue you. Don't let the vulnerability of being single cause you to rush something that you both are not ready for.

Take your time and allow God to be the captain of the relationship. If things are meant to be, time will tell; you will see God's hand in the relationship.

Prayer Affirmation

Father, in this season of singleness and waiting, please show us that we are merely preparing for what you have for us. Help us grow stronger in you. During this season, give us what to do and how to reach and encourage others. Help us to not focus on finding the mate but help us to grow deeper in love with you, your truths and your works.

Lord, help us to see our purpose. Help us to be a better witness of how your love changed our lives. I pray that our view of life will be an optimistic one. In our private times of devotion, speak to our hearts. Speak to that woman of God, that mighty intercessor that will bring forth divine healing. I'm calling for the midwives in the spirit to come forth, that every gift and seed planted will flourish. In this time of preparation, Lord, I ask that you fill the void. We will trust you, cultivate our friendship with you and tell others of the good news. Amen.

James 1:2-4; Philippians 4:6

Overcoming Difficulties

1. What is your process in dealing with challenges/issues?

   _____
   _____
   _____
   _____

2. Have you ever experienced a difficult time in life, if so on a scale of one to ten—ten being the biggest hardship you've ever faced in your life—where does this problem fall?

   _____
   _____
   _____

3. Sometimes our problems make us feel defeated. In what ways could this problem be a test of your faith?

   _____
   _____
   _____

Contentment, Not Envy

Contentment is a state of happiness and satisfaction.
(Merriam-Webster Dictionary)

Don't get "googly" eyes or "green eyes" at married couples. Things may look good on the outside, but you have no idea what they face as a couple. The children look well-groomed and well behaved, but you have no idea what it took for the parents to get them ready. Husband and wife may smile and laugh, but you'll never know the hurt they're dealing with. We are not to covet what someone else has; we should desire whatever God has for us. Every relationship is tailor made from the Creator himself.

Do you ever find yourself flipping through a couple's pictures, sighing over what seems to be perfect? Constantly rolling your eyes at their romantic gestures? Please be advised that feeling indifferent or envious over someone's relationship will not change your relationship status or feelings. We look at relationships and everything seems to be shining; in actuality, we don't have a single clue as to what is going on with that couple. We see what's happening on the surface, but if you only knew what that couple had to face day in and day out, it could definitely blow your mind. As it pertains to social media, that couple only allows us to see a portion of what they want us to see. We never see the bad and the ugly of the situation; we only see the lovely moments and positive outcomes of the marriage, which gives the illusion that everything is picture perfect with their relationship.

Envy or Nah?

Envying brings a lot of unwanted baggage, like discontentment, bitterness and resentment. It can also spiral you into depression. While you're focused on others and how they are living, you're losing focus on the most important person of this equation: Christ.

Instead of focusing on things that really matter like pleasing God, you're focusing on why you're not in a relationship and your own unhappiness. You should be content with what you have.

Prayer Affirmation

Lord, I ask that you touch my heart. Massage my heart of stone with your love, Lord.

I ask that you take this heart of hate and envy and create in me a clean heart and renew the right spirit in me. Show me how to accept my current season. Help me to look past my feelings and see the situation at face value. As I prepare my journey, show me how I can help others who may be dealing with this very issue. Lord, touch my mind, my heart and my soul; take out anything that is not like you. Amen.

Matthew 6:25-26; Philippians 4:12-13; Hebrews 13:5

Self-Check

Being Fully Content

1. In your own words what does it mean to be content? Are you content with your current state, if not what is something you would like to improve or change?
2. How do I want to feel on the inside?
3. When you're feeling discontent with yourself what do you do to escape the feeling?
4. How can I accept all I feel?
5. Romans 12:15(KJV) says, Rejoice with them that do rejoice… Think back to a situation where you had to rejoice with a friend or loved one and you weren't in a place of contentment or happiness? How hard was this for you? Can you be happy for someone else?
6. Do you feel self-conscious about what people think of you?
7. Is it difficult to make decisions?

Patience

> *Patience is the capacity to accept or tolerate delay, trouble, or suffering without getting angry or upset.*
> (Merriam-Webster Dictionary)

Someone once said that "patience is a virtue." Patience will literally try you; it'll push you to your limits. When seeking and praying for patience to deal with a certain situation, be prepared for any and everything. That is the very moment we are tried on every hand. In my season of singleness, I have been stretched to my fullest capacity. I've witnessed close friends get married, start a family and just living "the life." Here I am, yet standing here questioning my singleness, crying and asking, "Is it me? Was it something I said?" What I failed to realize is that there is a greater purpose awaiting me, if I just hold out.

If your singleness is uncontrolled, don't rush yourself into another relationship without fully healing from any and all past hurts. This is your time to prepare yourself for what God has in store for you. Don't be so anxious and place yourself in danger of rushing right into a destructive relationship.

Be careful for nothing; but in everything by prayer and supplication with thanksgiving let your requests be made known unto God. And the peace of God, which passeth all understanding, shall keep your hearts and minds through Christ Jesus. Philippians 4:6-7(KJV)

In this season, we must be patient with the will of God. Ask for God to show you the very thing you are called to be. Ask him to show you how to get to that place where he is calling you to. Sometimes, patience requires all of us. If you can pass the test, your patience will be renewed.

Prayer Affirmation

Lord, I ask that you continue to make me, mold me and shape me into what you want me to be. Stretch my faith so that I will be able to stand still on the salvation of the Lord. As I seek you, give me patience and temperance. Help me to be strong in my season of waiting. While I wait, I will serve you. Lord, endow me with wisdom, peace and love, so I may be that beacon light to someone else. Amen.

Psalms 75:2; Habakkuk 5:2-4; Romans 8:24-30

I Want Patience

1. What tests your patience the most? Why?
2. How would you define *patience*?
3. In what ways does God shows patience to you?
4. Why is it important for us to know that God is slow in His anger toward us?
5. In what ways does the fact that God waits for people to come to Him shows patience?

_____
_____
_____
_____
_____
_____
_____
_____
_____
_____
_____
_____

Hope Over Despair

Hope is a feeling of expectation and desire for a certain thing to happen.
(Merriam-Webster Dictionary)

Oftentimes, we see our friends and others on our social media timelines dating, engaged, married and/or expecting. We may question our very situation, not realizing that our hope is our blind faith, believing that something we've been praying for will come to pass in due season. I have hope; God's will shall be done in my life. Ladies, we must change our mindset.

We must stay focused and remember that just because it didn't manifest for you right away, doesn't mean that God has counted you out or has forgotten about you. We must have a heart of expectation, expecting God to complete the work in our lives. God may change your current state sooner than you think. Don't stop praying, don't give up. Lastly, don't stop hoping. God will definitely change your state. He will show up and show out in your future when you least expect it. He may not come when we want him to, but he will show up on time.

Despair is the complete loss or absence of hope.
(Merriam-Webster Dictionary)

We make declarations all the time; however, the question is: Do we believe it? A part of hope is believing. I encourage you to find your strength in Christ. A common setback is that we want the blessing without the work. The moment it doesn't come to fruition, we tend to lose all hope and faith. We have to remember that Rome wasn't built in a day. We must be prepared for whatever God has for us. In the season of waiting, focus your thoughts on God's Word.

Prayer Affirmation

Father, touch the minds and the hearts of your people. Allow them to see your will and plan for their lives. Help them to keep the faith, even when things don't seem to be going as planned. Remind them of your promises, Father God. Greater is on the other side of their release.

Lord, you are our hope, our strength and our peace. Endow us with more of your peace, your love, your joy and your hope. Guide us through all of the hurt and despair; give us understanding. Show us that greater is He that is in us. Show us that with you, all things are possible. Our hope is our blind faith in you. Where we are weak, Lord, make us strong.

Show us the way and guide our every thought. We ask this in the majestic name of Jesus. Amen.

Joshua 10:25; Job 6:8; Psalms 3:2-6, 147:11

Sealing Your Hope

1. How has God fulfilled His promises in the past in your life?

   _____
   _____
   _____
   _____

2. What would your life look like if God was in full control?

   _____
   _____
   _____
   _____

3. How has God shown that He cares in your life?

   _____
   _____
   _____
   _____

Identity Crisis

Identity Crisis is a state of confusion in an institution or organization regarding its nature or direction.
(Merriam-Webster Dictionary)

Who am I?

If you look at today's society, there are so many depictions of how we as ladies should dress and how we should carry ourselves. While you're in self-discovery mode, you've discovered that the life you've lived and the path you've taken is not your own. You've been living a counterfeit life. We've compromised ourselves for way too long. It's time for us to come out from among them. (2 Corinthians 6:17) (NIV)

Do you know who you are? Most importantly, do you know whose you are? We're so caught up in the world's way of living, it's even hard to identify a genuinely chaste woman. Our apparel and how we carry ourselves should be modest; we shouldn't try to keep up with Jones'.

Mirror, Mirror

Mirror, Mirror on the wall, who's the bravest of them all? Who's the prettiest?
Growing up, my father would tell me I'm beautiful; so when I heard it for the first time from a guy, it wouldn't excite me to the point where I'd fall head over heels over him. Ladies, we must to return to

our rightful place. The woman is to be loved and adored. We are royalty.

Have you truly looked at yourself in the mirror? On a daily basis, you look in a mirror to fix your hair, get ready for work or school. You should look in the mirror and tell your reflection that you are beautiful, you are amazing and talented. Write that affirmation on a sticky note and put it in a visible place such as your headboard, your desk at work or even make it your screensaver on your computer. When others try to tell you that you're not beautiful, you can easily refer back to these affirmations.

We have looked up to secular artists, models and personalities for far too long. It's time to call forth the Proverbs 31 woman within, the "Model Woman" who exemplifies what the Word is saying. Proverbs 31:1(KJV) says, *"Who can find a virtuous woman? for her price is far above rubies."* Ladies, you are worth far more than these men will have you to believe. *For I am fearfully and **wonderfully** made: marvelous are thy works; and that my soul knoweth right well.* Psalms 139:14(KJV).

To answer your question, *"Who am I?"* You are a virtuous woman. You are strength. You are crafty. You are wise.

Prayer Affirmation

Father God, forgive me for setting my heart on things of this world and defining myself by these earthly standards and skills. I repent for not thinking on the things of you, for becoming consumed and distracted by those around me. Take away every thought and desire that does not line up with your will. Holy Spirit, make known to me the reality of who my Father is. Lord, I thank you, for I am precious, pursued, honored and loved. Because of your precious spirit that lives inside of me, I am forever thankful for your faithfulness toward me. I declare that I am a child of the King, and I will not grow weary. Asking, declaring and receiving it in Jesus' name. Amen.

Jeremiah 1:5, 1 Corinthians 12:27, Ephesians 4:22-27

Identity Check

1. What is *identity*?

2. What are some of the false identities that people around you cling to?

3. Why is it important to know what your identity is?

4. 1 Peter 2:9 touches on a few of the ways the Bible describes identity. Can you think of anymore?

Holiness, Not Sin

For I am the Lord your God: ye shall therefore sanctify yourselves, and ye shall be holy; for I am holy: neither shall ye defile yourselves with any manner of creeping thing that creepeth upon the earth.
Leviticus 11:44

We are commanded to be holy. This is a command not just for the Israelites, this command applies to us also today. To live a holy life, you must not conform to the sinful ways of the world. Holiness is a requirement and standard for godly living.

Follow peace with all men, and holiness, without which no man shall see the Lord. Hebrews 12:14.

God, in the very beginning, gave us the recipe for living a complete life in Him. He said, *be holy as I am holy*. We must take on the lifestyle of our Savior. Holiness isn't just a state of being; it's a lifestyle. To live a holy life in a world that magnifies sin, you must turn from your wicked ways. Living a holy life is to put off your old self and walk into the newness of God. Ladies, we were created to be like God in true righteousness and holiness.

Holy, Set Apart

When I think of living holy, **1 Peter 1:13-16** comes to mind:
Wherefore gird up the loins of your mind, be sober, and hope to the end for the grace

that is to be brought unto you at the revelation of Jesus Christ; As obedient children, not fashioning yourselves according to the former lusts in your ignorance: But as he which hath called you is holy, so be ye holy in all manner of conversation; Because it is written, Be ye holy; for I am holy.

To be holy means to be separate. Just like how oil and water cannot and will not mix, as children of God, we must not mix or intermingle with things that would take us off our square. We must not allow others to influence us to lose our rightful place in God.

How do we live a holy life? In order to effectively address this question, we must truly understand what *holiness* means. To be holy means to be set apart and separate from all sin and evil. God is holy and He calls for us to be holy. In our time of courting, we must remember that without holiness, no man shall see the Lord. We must follow the basic principles that God has laid out before you. We must draw boundaries and hold standards that allows us to remain focused on that goal, *marriage,* without having anything to hold you back.

Prayer Affirmation

Father, touch the minds and hearts of your people. Help us to be more like you. Lord, you are a holy God; make us more like you. Lord, give us a heart of love like yours. Give us a mind to think like you. Help your daughters to be vessels of honor in your name.

Stir up the gift of discernment within us so we may be able to see the good and the evil. Lord, guide us in life and as we prepare for our mates. Hide us in you so we may be found at the appointed time by the one you created for us, Father God.

Psalms 119:9; 2 Corinthians 7:1; Hebrews 12:14; 1 Peter 1:15-16

Holiness, not Sin

1. What are some thing(s) that are keeping you from being holy?

   _____
   _____
   _____
   _____
   _____
   _____
   _____

2. What is separating you from receiving all that God has for you?

   _____
   _____
   _____
   _____
   _____
   _____
   _____
   _____
   _____
   _____

Guarding Your Heart

Keep thy heart with all diligence; for out of it are the issues of life.
Put away from thee a froward mouth, and perverse lips put far from thee.
Let thine eyes look right on, and let thine eyelids look straight before thee.
Ponder the path of thy feet, and let all thy ways be established.
Turn not to the right hand nor to the left: remove thy foot from evil.
Proverbs 4:23-27 (KJV)

Proverbs 4:23 tells us to keep our hearts with all diligence. Be cautious with what information you share with others, especially when meeting new people. Guard your heart by filtering out the things that doesn't apply to you, knowing how and when to speak. Let us take a look at Philippians 4:6-7(KJV).

Be careful for nothing; but in everything by prayer and supplication with thanksgiving let your requests be made known unto God.

We must make our requests known to God, have faith and believe that those things will come to pass in God's timing. Do not allow certain things into your space or thoughts. In all things, seek God and all of his righteousness. Seek God for direction on making the right decisions and what you are purposed to do. If you believe, what you asked for will come to pass. Give Him all the praise! When praises go up, blessings will come down.

And the peace of God, which passeth all understanding, shall keep your hearts and minds through Christ Jesus. Philippians 4:7(KJV)

The faith in knowing that God will honor your requests allows peace to rest over you. That peace shall be your portion that'll keep you until that appointed time of supernatural release. Ladies, when meeting and courting, we need to exercise wisdom in our decisions. Again, as I've stated before, we need the gift of discernment.

Prayer Affirmation

Lord, I ask that you lift up the standard to protect my fellow sisters. Touch their hearts and heal the hurt and broken places; remove everything that is not like you from their minds and hearts. Your word says that a contrite spirit and a broken heart you will not scorn. You are our healer and our deliverer, so we trust you to touch, heal and deliver every heart that is held captive to past decisions, relationships and situations. Lord, we have faith that you will exceed our expectations. In this very moment, we declare that we are free from all hurt, guilt and pain. We ask that you build a hedge of protection around our hearts and awaken our gift of discernment so we may be able to see the good and evil that presents itself, in Jesus' name, amen.

Psalms 73:26; Proverbs 4:23; John 14:27

Guarding Your Heart

1. How does guarding your mouth keep your heart pure?

2. How does guarding your eyes keep your heart pure?

3. How does guarding your feet keep your heart pure?

4. What choices will you make this week to guard your heart?

Blocking the Noise: Deceptive Voices

Deception is the act of deceiving.
(Merriam-Webster Dictionary)

God has been dealing with me in dreams. Recently, I had a dream concerning deception. In this dream, I was in a relationship although the extent of that relationship wasn't clear. However, I was riding around in luxury vehicles, shopping and being wined and dined. Throughout this dream, I was happy, experiencing what I thought to be true love; however, I didn't know that this was all part of the enemy's plan. The closer you are to your destiny, purpose, and most certainly, your promise, counterfeits will surface.

Counterfeit is made in exact imitation of something valuable or important with the intention to deceive or defraud.
(Merriam-Webster Dictionary)

Many opportunities will surface, but we must be in tune with God's Word and His voice so we can identify the impostor. There are situations designed to take us off our square and frustrate us. How will it frustrate us? By presenting false hope and counterfeit experiences after you've fallen prey to the snare of that situation or the individual, now you're ready to shut out everyone else's thoughts or concerns out of fear you stay reluctantly. Before we say, "God said" or "God instructed me," we must first realize and understand that the enemy has a voice and speaks to us. We must seek God for clarity before totally submitting ourselves to something that could possibly be damnable to our souls.

In this dream, I was under the impression that I met my soulmate, the one for me. It wasn't until I woke up that I sought interpretation and understood the meaning of the dream. The thing that looks appealing and seems suitable is merely a deceptive vice designed to take you completely out of the will of God. It'll take more than just a severance of ties to rekindle your relationship with God. Ladies, be careful who you allow in your circle; we must stay focused. Be careful of what you confess to be of God. That could be your flesh speaking. Just because you both may have things in common doesn't make him your future spouse. You do not want to miss what God has for you for a "Bozo," someone you're not even meant to be with.

Prayer Affirmation

Father God, I pray that you would touch my dear sisters. Show them the way; keep them from all hurt, harm and danger. Stir up the gift that's within. Block out any noise that would keep us from hearing you ever so clearly. I ask that you drown out the voice of every tempter that comes to distract us from our divine purpose. Lord, open our eyes and ears so we may clearly see and hear what it is that you are showing us concerning deception. Lord, if there be anyone in our lives that shouldn't be, show us. We ask these things in your Son Jesus' name. Thank God, amen.

Matthew 14:28-31, Hebrew 12:12, 1 John 2:15

Tuning Out Deceptive Voices

1. Have I laid down my will and sought only the will and purposes of the Father in all areas of my life?

   _____
   _____
   _____
   _____

2. Am I being washed daily by the constant application of the Word of God?

   _____
   _____
   _____
   _____

3. Are there some relationships I've allowed that have caused me to be distracted from my true purpose?

   _____
   _____
   _____
   _____

Overcoming Rejection

Rejection is to refuse to accept (someone) as a spouse, or friend; rebuff.
(Merriam-Webster Dictionary)

I've had my share of rejections, whether it was from a university, a job, friends or potential mates. Rejection is being refused for whatever reason, sometimes with little to no explanation. Over the years, I faced rejection based on looks or because I wasn't the type of woman that would do any and everything (if you catch my drift). As we walk with Christ, we have to accept some rejections and move forward. Some are God-ordained rejections to get your attention.

In our previous section, we asked the Lord to help block out the noise and voice of deception. In this section, we want to deal with the spirit of rejection. Oftentimes, the true intent of the rejecter is to get you in a place of weakness. Once rejected, you could dumb yourself down to their level and they'll be the one on top while you're constantly being punched on every side.

A person can take only so much rejection before it takes a toll on them. Whether it is large or small, it plays a huge part on you mentally. Rejection hurts more than we anticipate at times. Why is that? Rejection affects us the same way as physical pain. Rejection has no boundaries; it can invade personal space, romantic and job situations.

It's a form of distancing someone from a group or giving someone the "cold shoulder." For instance, guys who are not willing to wait, settle or compromise will reject you instantly because of their lack of patience.

Rejection plays a huge role on the emotions. We must get a handle on them and grow tough skin, because someone will say or do something that will offend you. We must realize that rejection is a clear sign that you aren't meant to be in the company of some people. God will show you who is for you and who isn't; but it takes a strong prayer life to be able to hear and accept the things of God.

Prayer is our way of communication with the Father. Through prayer, we can hear directly from Him. Whenever you feel like you're being rejected, just turn to the Father, the only One who can mend your brokenness.

Prayer Affirmation

Lord, as you mend and heal our broken hearts, shield my sisters from all manners of rejection and hurt. Father, I may not understand this situation, but I do understand your goodness to me. Help me replace the fears threatening to consume me with truth. I know you love me; you are for me, and I absolutely can trust you with all of my heart. In Jesus' name, amen.

Romans 8:28; 2 Corinthians 12:9

Questions you should ask when facing rejection

1. How were you rejected?
   _____
   _____
   _____
   _____
   _____

2. How did it make you feel?
   _____
   _____
   _____
   _____
   _____

3. What's one thing you could do better?
   _____
   _____
   _____
   _____
   _____

Breaking the Stronghold of Lust

"So flee youthful passions and pursue righteousness, faith, love, and peace, along with those who call on the Lord from a pure heart."
2 Timothy 2:22 ESV

*L*ust *is usually intense or unbridled* **desire**.
(Merriam-Webster Dictionary)

Second Timothy 2:22 reminds us to flee from those things that cause us to lust and to fall back into the pits of our past. We must realize and understand that these attacks are from the enemy.

For though we walk in the flesh, we do not war after the flesh:
(For the weapons of our warfare are not carnal, but mighty through God to the pulling down of strongholds;)Casting down imaginations, and every high thing that exalteth itself against the knowledge of God, and bringing into captivity every thought to the obedience of Christ;
2 Corinthians 10:3-5 KJV

Let's walk through this particular passage of Scripture: **for though we walk in the flesh, we do not war after the flesh**

Yes, we walk in the flesh as mortal men, but our battle is out of this world. Our battle is spiritual. We cannot combat these issues with our hands; we must combat through prayer. Day and night, the enemy is seeking whom he can devour. Therefore, we must pray strategically, asking the Lord to cover us in His blood daily.

And when he putteth forth his own sheep, he goeth before them, and the sheep follow him: for they know his voice. And a stranger will they not follow, but will flee from him: for they know not the voice of strangers.
John 10:4-5 KJV

How to Break the Stronghold of Lust

First things first: we must acknowledge that we have a problem. We constantly battle with bad thoughts and overindulging. It may not seem like a big deal and we may think that we've gotten over it, but we must first give it to God.

1. **Observe yourself**: The first step to overcome a stronghold is acknowledging that you have a problem. Look at yourself in the mirror of the Word. What do you see? Take time to observe your thoughts, actions and speech. Be honest with yourself. Judge yourself.

   Judge not, that ye be not judged. For with what judgment ye judge, ye shall be judged: and with what measure ye mete, it shall be measured to you again. And why beholdest thou the mote that is in thy brother's eye, but considerest not the beam that is in thine own eye? Or how wilt thou say to thy brother, Let me pull out the mote out of thine eye; and, behold, a beam is in thine own eye? Thou hypocrite, first cast out the beam out of thine own eye; and then shalt thou see clearly to cast out the mote out of thy brother's eye. Matthew 7:1-5

2. **Deliverance is available**: Only the power of God can break the stronghold of sin.

Once you've observed yourself, you can ask God to remove the things that have you bound. In doing so, God can show you the right and wrong things in your life. Your natural mind may see nothing wrong, but the Spirit of God will tell you otherwise. We must ask for a deeper love for God's Word and His will.

3. **God has given you a will - use it!** According to Romans 12:1-3, we are instructed to renew our minds. When we align our will with the will of God, all things are possible. Oftentimes, when we think we're doing the right things, we're really going off our moral compass and not what God has instructed for us to do. Make a decision to turn from your old ways.
4. **Make reading the Word a daily habit**: His Word is the medicine that will set and keep you free. Take it like medicine: regularly and in the right dosage. Set aside time daily to read the Word of God.

Prayer Affirmation

Father, please touch the hearts and minds of your daughters. Remove every thought that comes to distract us. Allow us to see things through your eyes. When tempting thoughts arise, let a song of praise quickly flood our soul so we may think on those things and not the things of our flesh. Lord, help us to walk upright, to filter our thoughts and deny the desires of the flesh. In this inhumane world we live in, give us strength to endure.

Lord we thank you, and we bless your name in advance for all you're about to do for us. Amen.

Breaking the Stronghold of Lust

1. Identify your triggers that cause you to have lustful thoughts.

   _____
   _____
   _____
   _____

2. What do you do when you feel yourself slipping?

   _____
   _____
   _____
   _____

3. How can you keep yourself from lustful thoughts or situations?

   _____
   _____
   _____
   _____

Sure, Why Not? What Harm Could It Do?

God reveals, prepares or warns me through dreams. Referring back to our previous section about deception, we must be careful who we connect with. We do not know the true intent of the person, nor do we know what they're really connecting with us for.

In this dream, I was in an intimate relationship with a man. Everything was going fine early on in the dream. At some point, I blacked out and all I could see was myself being carried out by this male figure. Again, I was happy; everything was going well. But in a matter of minutes, things turned for the worst. I could've been dead at this point, but I was rushed to the hospital. How could this be? How could the one person I loved, who made me smile and completed me, harm me?

As the dream continued, I was in a hospital bed and the same guy came back into the room at first to assure me that everything was great. He kissed me, and within minutes, once again he attempted to do me harm. The first time was to only hurt me; the second time was meant to kill me. Luckily, I was able to scream out for help.

Ashley, why are you telling this story? To show you that

deceptive individuals will and can harm you without even blinking. Please understand the importance of having a relationship with God through prayer and supplication so you'll be sensitive to His warnings.

And a stranger will they not follow, but will flee from him: for they know not the voice of strangers.
John 10:5 (KJV)

Had I not established a relationship with God, more than likely, I would not have received this warning. Of course, several godly men and women have spoken a word over my life concerning my husband and that he's coming. Being in my feelings, I spoke into the atmosphere that I was giving up. I was going to just date an ex or just some random dude until my husband comes. I literally walked down my stairs grinning, but God had other plans for me. That very night, He spoke to me in this dream. Ultimately, I realized that this was a clear indication that I needed to wait until the Lord sends my other half.

All things are lawful unto me, but all things are not expedient: all things are lawful for me, but I will not be brought under the power of any.
1 Corinthians 6:12 KJV

Just because something is technically legal doesn't mean that it's spiritually appropriate. If I went around doing whatever I thought I could get by with, I'd be a slave to my whims.
1 Corinthians 6:12 MSG

Ladies, just because something can pacify or satisfy us until that appointed time doesn't mean that we should take part in it. I know it gets hard to see others around you in relationships, married with children while you're still single without a single prospect. Let me say this: we all have prospects designed by God, but it's when we get in our own way, trying to make things happen that we miss out on the one God has for us.

Hang in there. Keep yourself occupied with productive activities like writing, reading, praying or being creative while you wait on God to send your blessing. That "Sure, why not?" list is not the list that you want to be on. That's the moment when the enemy uses your weakness against you. You may fall into something you may not recover from.

Prayer Affirmation

Father, in our season of singleness, grant us patience and wisdom to know when situations and people are not for us. As we embark upon our journeys, strengthen us to push past our fleshly desires. When we don't understand your will for our lives, help us to understand. Lord, protect us from the wolves in sheep's clothing, and help us to see people for who they really are. Show us the intent behind every connection.

Psalms 27:13-14; Isaiah 40:31; 2 Peter 3:9

Have you ever had a dream and time passed and you felt like you were reliving a moment? Some call it Deja Vu I simply say that God is trying to get our attention. Growing up I remember my mother would tell me not to do certain things but when she wasn't paying attention I would commit the act. Have you ever experienced God sending you a warning but you went ahead and committed the act anyhow? What was the outcome? What did you learn from the experience?

_____

_____

_____

_____

_____

_____

_____

_____

_____

_____

_____

Single and Loving it

The first step to overcoming the struggle of being single is accepting your singleness. Instead of looking at it as a curse or being lonely, treat this as a time to be about your Father's business without any restraints. Use this time to prepare for marriage and fall in love with yourself again. In your time of waiting, your focus should be on fulfilling your purpose and promise to God.

Throughout my time of singleness, I've *learned* things about myself that I had to get a handle of. There were areas of weakness I had that could possibly scare my mate away. In order to grow, you must let go of some habits.

> **Habit** *is a settled tendency or usual manner of behavior.*
> (Merriam-Webster Dictionary)

Our main task is to seek God like never before and focus on growing our relationship with Christ. I know I've mentioned it before, "*Seek ye first the kingdom of God, and his righteousness; and all these things shall be added unto you.*" (Matthew 6:33) *(KJV)* When you focus on the things that matter most, God will certainly open doors for you and give you the desires of your heart. Your focus should shift towards ministry and what you could do to enhance the ministry, which comes after you seek God for direction. During this time of singleness, of course, you deal with thoughts of loneliness and the desire to date; **we must find comfort in knowing that God will in due season bless us with the mate that he has designed for us. We must not become so focused on the finished product but in fact work in your purpose allowing God to send your purpose mate. Sister's stay focused on God and watch Him blow your mind, every desire shall come to pass but you must be in position, stay ready so you don't have to get ready.** Sometimes, our desire causes depression. I've experienced all the above.

What helped me? Abiding in God's presence. Every time the enemy would try to remind me of my relationship status, I would combat it with prayer. Even when I was down and lost in my emotions, I still had the strength to remind myself that I am wonderfully and fearfully made (Psalms 139:14). I am above and not beneath, that I'm on *special order*. Oftentimes, we stop at the pain but never push past the emotional strain. If you fight for your happiness while single, I promise you will rise to the occasion every time. Just like a **bricklayer,** you take brick by brick and construct whatever it is you're commissioned to build. We deal with rejection, depression, loneliness, just to name a few. Are your bricks from the spiritual aspect of hindrances? You have to break down those walls and free yourself from things that are holding you hostage.

One of the fondest things I've heard is that we must serve while waiting. We must tear down those things that have held us captive, find our place in ministry and serve diligently.

Prayer Affirmation

Lord, help us to keep our minds on you. When those moments of temptation arise, Lord I ask that you keep my sisters. Keep us hidden in you, that no hurt, harm or danger would come against us. Lord, please protect us daily from the very snare of the enemy. When we begin to compare ourselves to others, Lord show us what you would have for us to do and to be. When distractions come our way, Lord remove them far from us. Bind the hand of the enemy even now, that would distract us from our destiny. In Jesus' name, amen.

1 Corinthians 7:32-35; 2 Corinthians 6:14

Self-Check

Sometimes we have the tendency to hold onto situations longer than we need to. Write a letter to someone who has done you wrong. Discuss what they did and how it made you feel.

_____
_____
_____
_____
_____
_____
_____
_____
_____
_____
_____
_____
_____
_____
_____
_____
_____
_____

See No Evil, Hear No Evil, Speak No Evil: Overcoming Temptations

Keep thy heart with all diligence; for out of it are the issues of life. Put away from thee a froward mouth, and perverse lips put far from thee. Let thine eyes look right on, and let thine eyelids look straight before thee.
Proverbs 4:23-25

We must be mindful of the things we watch and listen to, and most importantly, what we say. Especially in this era of modern technology and social media, we must guard our eye and ears gates. I'll be completely honest with you: it doesn't matter who you are, what church you attend or how long you've been saved. Temptation can find you; the enemy doesn't care who he attacks because his main goal is to seek and devour you.

Temptation is the act of tempting or the state of being tempted especially to evil.
(Merriam-Webster Dictionary)

Transparent moment: growing up in a Christian household with my mother and father, I attended Sunday school, Sunday worship, Prayer and Bible Band, and Friday night evangelism teaching. I never hung around the wrong crowd. I went to school, came home and never spent the night at any of my friends' houses.

I was over a relative's house with my cousins. Growing up, we would have several competitions and on this particular night, we were trying to see who could stay up the longest. I could never win as I would be the first one to fall asleep. No matter how hard I tried, I could never outlast my cousins or sister.

Disclaimer: HBO after dark is not for children. I woke up late in the midnight hour. I found myself staring at the screen trying to understand what I was seeing. I wasn't at the age to learn about the "birds and bees" just yet. Over a period of time, whenever I would stay over, it became a cycle of trying to understand all that was going on. It wasn't until my eighth grade health class that I began to understand. I battled with the temptation, and actually was consumed by pornography for years. I had to seek God, tune out all of the noise and gain an understanding of this issue. It seemed like every time I was healed and delivered, the temptation would come back stronger than the last. You will have moments of weakness until you give that situation over to the Lord completely. We must kill our flesh daily and flee from the things that would tempt us.

My prayer is that my moment of transparency will open your eyes and heart to realize and understand that temporary satisfaction pulls you deeper into sin and farther away from your Father. The bigger the wedge, the harder it is for you to get back to your rightful place.

The enemy has literally peeped into your future and he see the great exploits you will do in the name of the Father. If he can take you off your square, he feels that he has won. What he doesn't realize is that what he meant for evil, the Lord will use to build your testimony. It shall work for your good (Romans 8:28). We all may have faced similar situations, but our testimony is important for our release. We must fight until the end. Let God arise in your situation and the enemy shall scatter. God is able to bring you out. Don't stop at the altar; continue to walk in your deliverance. It doesn't end after the prayer; it is carried out throughout the rest of your life.

Prayer Affirmation

Lord, touch our minds and heart. You instructed us in your word to protect our heart, eyes and our lips that we speak without perverse tongues. Do an inside job on my heart and mind and take out anything that is not like you. I confess with my mouth that I have rebelled against your word; I've brought shame to your name. I pray that every life will be changed for your glory. Complete the process of healing and deliverance in our lives. In Jesus' name, amen.

Proverbs 1:10; Matthew 26:41; Luke 4:8; 1 Corinthians 6:18; Ephesians 5:11, 12

Overcoming Temptation

1. How do you feel when you give into temptation?

   _____
   _____
   _____
   _____
   _____
   _____
   _____

2. How can we respond wisely to temptation?

   _____
   _____
   _____
   _____
   _____
   _____
   _____
   _____
   _____

Realize You Have Something to Offer

Freedom is the absence of necessity, coercion, or constraint in choice or action.
(Merriam-Webster Dictionary)

Now the Lord is that Spirit: and where the Spirit of the Lord is, there is liberty.
2 Corinthians 3:17

Oftentimes, we hold onto issues from our past which ultimately hinder us from obtaining all that God has for us. Things seem to be going perfectly, and then something is triggered from our past. Maybe you're scrolling through your timeline and you see memories of what you used to be involved in. I know we hear all the time that we shouldn't cut people out of our lives and when we do cut them out, we must do it with care and I totally agree. When we make the choice to move on, we must do it with the understanding that we cannot blame ourselves solely for why things went south.

Oftentimes, people really can't see your worth. You must realize is that you truly have something to offer and that you're on the brink of something spectacular happening in your life. You have more to offer than you realize. We don't give ourselves enough credit sometimes. The saying is true: *we are our worst critics*. Even after a bad breakup or just an ending of a relationship in general, we oftentimes forget that we, too, are as great as when we were in a relationship. We should use that same energy to embrace greater.

I look at each friendship and acquaintance as a learning opportunity. From there, I can see and evaluate what I could've done better. It is difficult for us to see that we have more to offer, that we are strong because of the drive for companionship. In your season of singleness, identify what it is that you're passionate about. From there, you should be able to identify what you can offer in your next season.

Prayer of Affirmation

Lord, I thank you for the gifts that you have birthed within me. I ask that you heal me from the hurt of my past. Help me to see my fullest potential. Lord, open my eyes so I may see all that I have within. Help my unbelief and remove any doubt I may have. Help me to stop comparing myself to others, for we were all created differently. We are set apart from others. Lord, help us to realize that even in dating, we have so much to offer that eyes cannot see it all. Lord, take our prayer life to another level in you. In this next season, show us what you would have for us to do. Lord, continue to drive me to be all that you have called me to be. We thank you in advance for all that you're doing in our lives. Amen.

What do you have to offer?

1. What am I bringing to the table in the relationship?

   _____
   _____
   _____
   _____
   _____
   _____
   _____

2. What actually brings you contentment in your own life right now?

   _____
   _____
   _____
   _____
   _____
   _____
   _____
   _____
   _____

Forgiveness

To give up resentment of or claim requital.
(Merriam-Webster Dictionary)

Oftentimes, we view forgiveness as a hard pill to swallow. When we decide to forgive others, we are setting ourselves free. I have learned to forgive. Walking around, holding onto the hurt, upset from past situations and relationships were getting me nowhere. I've been hurt by a person who I trusted, someone I thought had my best intentions. For some time, I relived the pain and hurt. I hoped that the person would just come forth; the damage was done and all I wanted was that apology and reasoning for all the hurt that was caused. Time passed by and that healing never came.

Instead of reliving the moment, I want to talk to you on how to forgive. It is a hard task, but in the end, the freedom is well worth it.

It's a hard thing to do—to completely let go of something painful and forgive the person who may or may not have realized what they did. At my angriest point, I was convinced the person who hurt me did it with cruel intentions. I felt not a shred of compassion; just unadulterated pain and rage. That's when I realized that they probably felt the same way I did. But because of their ego, they couldn't admit they were wrong. I never attribute these actions to the person. Not everyone is bad or has bad intentions; these things come from misunderstandings of a particular situation. When we forgive others for the hurt they've caused, it's not for them, it's solely for us. We must release all of the hurt and the people who let us down. I acknowledge that we're all humans and we make mistakes.

In making mistakes, we can also misconstrue a situation because of the lack of understanding.

Forgive Me, Forgive Me Not

How did I forgive when it was hard? I came to this realization: No one ever gets to the end of their life and thinks, "I wish I stayed angry longer." They generally say one of three things: "I'm sorry," "I forgive you," or "I love you."

After taking time to heal myself, I decided to cut out the middleman of time. I now set boundaries to take better care of me, but I'll never regret that I've forgiven.

Prayer Affirmation

Lord, I thank you for your gift of forgiveness. Your only Son loved me enough to come to Earth and experience the worst pain imaginable so I could be forgiven. Your mercy flows to me in spite of my faults and failures. Lord, help me to forgive others as you have extended forgiveness to me. Your Word says to "clothe yourselves with love, which binds us all together in perfect harmony." (Colossians 3:14) Help me demonstrate unconditional love today, even to those who hurt me. I understand that although I feel scarred, my emotions don't have to control my actions. Father, may your sweet words saturate my mind and direct my thoughts. Help me release the hurt and begin to love as Jesus loves. You teach us to "let the peace that comes from Christ rule in our hearts." (Colossians 3:15) When I forgive in words, allow your Holy Spirit to fill my heart with peace. Above all, Father, I am thankful, not just this week, but always. I praise you for the work you are doing in my life, for teaching and perfecting my faith. In Jesus' name, amen.

Matthew 6:14-15, Acts 3:19, Ephesians 4:31-3

Forgiveness

1. Why do you think it is difficult to forgive those who hurt you?
2. Read Luke 5:17-26, the healing of the paralytic. What does this passage imply about the relationship between forgiveness and healing?
3. How could extending forgiveness heal a relationship? How might it heal the other person? How might it heal you?
4. Respond to the following quote: "When you refuse to forgive, you are giving the person who hurt you once the privilege of hurting you all over again—in your memory." Do you agree or disagree? Why or why not?
5. Share an example from your own experience when refusing to forgive hurt you.

What Glitters Isn't Gold: Relationship Goals

Social media and its depiction of relationships will have you falling for the hype of believing what you see. Oftentimes, we compare our relationship goals to those of celebrities, friends and others we see. Ladies, let's face it: your soulmate isn't going to be comparable to that what we see online. Our perfect match is created by God Himself. We are on special order; at the appointed time, God will reveal us to our mate. Oftentimes, God deals with us in dreams, visions and the Word; but we must remember to not let what we see determine how we look at things.

I've found myself time after time watching love stories, and after it's all said and done, I would imagine myself in a relationship similar to the one I saw on the big screen. I would meet new people and try to live out what I saw.

The biggest mistake I've made was looking at one's relationship, taking note of what I liked and adding it to my list. *Wrong!* You never know what they've endure behind closed doors. They smile in the videos and you see all of the flowers, but you have no idea what they go through on a daily basis. I hear my brothers testify all the time how they got so lost in God that they ultimately found their mate in God.

Our focus shouldn't be on a relationship; it should be focused on growing in God, identifying what our God-given purpose is and walking in it.

Prayer Affirmation

Lord, help us to not focus on the relationships we see. When we see others post their love stories, help us to not covet and be swayed by what we see. Lord, help us to only desire that tailor-made relationship that you have for me. Let us be focused on developing a relationship with you above all. Help us to know who we are in you so that when our significant other comes, we will stand confident with our heads held high, knowing that we are someone's "good thing." Thank you, Father for shining your love on us. Amen.

Self-Check

In living in a time where relationships we see are highly publicized, what are some things that you would keep to yourself while dating, courting, engaged or married?

Fear: Reject Fearful Thoughts

Fear is to be afraid of; except with alarm.
(Merriam-Webster Dictionary)

One of the most common things we as singles experience is the fear of possibly never meeting that special someone. We fear that we will never reach our fullest potential or that we've missed our moment. We fear that no one will ever notice us. That was me, once upon a time. I was held captive by the fear that I would always end up alone and friendless. I walked around feeling less than what I truly was. I realized that in my moments of loneliness, God can speak and impart what He needs for you to do. You can hear better from God. Ladies, this is the prime time for you to get yourself together.

Do not be anxious about anything, but in everything, by prayer and petition, with thanksgiving, present your requests to God. And the peace of God, which transcends all understanding, will guard your hearts and your minds in Christ Jesus.
Philippians 4:6, 7 NIV

The Bible instructs us to guard our hearts and minds in Christ. We must not be anxious for those things that we have yet to obtain, but rather seek God through prayer, petitioning Him for everything we need. The peace of God will rest on us. We have to stop adoring and swooning over those online, publicized relationships.

You may have fought with fear, but I declare that after this day, you will no longer hold yourself hostage with the fear of not being enough.

Prayer Affirmation

Father, when my sisters fall back into that place of fear, remind them that they are wonderfully and fearfully made. Help your children to trust in your timing and in the process. Help your children to live a life free of fear. Remind your children of your Word, that you did not give us the spirit of fear, but of power, and of love, and of a sound mind. Amen.

Self-Check

We know that fear is a tactic of the enemy to keep us from reaching our fullest potential. Why are you stuck in that place of fear?

_____
_____
_____
_____
_____
_____
_____
_____
_____
_____
_____
_____
_____
_____
_____
_____
_____
_____
_____

Stop Criticizing Yourself

Criticizing is to find fault with: point out the faults.
(Merriam-Webster Dictionary)

As a young woman growing up, oftentimes I have compared myself to others: the way I look, the way I dress and how I should carry myself due to how society has presented the "average woman." I'm a thinker who loves to sit and write out my ideas. I would write things out and turn around to see someone with the very same idea. Instead of pursuing it, I'd throw it away. Many times, we hurt ourselves and are only doing ourselves a disservice by not acting on those things we have dreamt of. We are not to be like anyone else but the one who God created us to be. If we would just step back and look at ourselves, we were created uniquely in His image. Each of us has our own identity; how we manage to take care of it is totally on us.

I believe that we should carry ourselves in a way that not only is acceptable but keeps us happy. If you love getting your nails done and dressing nicely, that's something you should attribute to being happy. Show yourself compassion; stop beating yourself up because you aren't where others are. Just because you haven't arrived doesn't mean that you should give up on yourself. You have to be excited even if no one else cares. You have to do it for yourself. When you are building your brand, you can't compare yourself to others. Each us has our own gift and destiny.

I'm guilty of constantly pulling out the negatives and using them as jokes, poking fun at my faults. For years, in order to feel comfortable I thought I had to tear myself down. Did you know that many cases of depression are self-inflicted? We sometimes bring on a number of these issues due to dissatisfaction with ourselves. We daily fight the idea of not being like everyone else, and not fitting in with societal norms so much so that we lose focus on the real issue. We must be content and carry a positive attitude throughout our day.

Prayer Affirmation

Lord, I know that I am my own worst enemy. Help me to think positive and according to your word. When the world paints a picture of how we should appear, help us to remain constant in your Word. A virtuous woman is a crown to her husband; but she that maketh ashamed is as rottenness in his bones. Amen.

Self-Check

Four times to start loving your life instead of criticizing yourself

1. Speak to yourself as you'd speak to someone you love and want to encourage.
2. See yourself as loved ones see you.
3. Make a list of things that you appreciate about yourself.

Remember that you are human, and that you are imperfect.

Prayer Journal Prompt

Draw a line down the length of your journal page to create 2 columns. In the left column, make a list of the criticisms you level at yourself most often. In the right column, for each criticism, write a statement of encouragement — something you might say to someone else in that situation.

Criticism	Positive Affirmations

Can You Fix It? Yes, You Can!

There was a popular children's show that my sister and I would watch growing up.

The song in this show would get us so amped!

"*Bob the Builder, can we fix it?*" Affectionately, we would scream back, "Yes, we can!" That was Bob's attitude concerning life's matters and everything he faced. We ought to have that same attitude. Sometimes, in life we go through minute situations. At other times, life gives you lemons. No matter what the situation may be, we should be able to look at it and say that we can fix it. How do we fix our lives problems? Through prayer and fasting, we can combat anything.

I have been through many obstacles through life. Some were taxing, to the point that I should've honestly lost my mind. It was God's grace and mercy that kept me. Even when things seem unbearable, if you turn those things over to God, He'll not only fix it, but He'll heal the hurt and mend the brokenness.

"Cast your burden on the Lord [release it] and He will sustain and uphold you; He will never allow the righteous to be shaken (slip, fall, fail)."
Psalms 55:22

By casting all of your cares and burdens on the Lord, that heaviness would then be released. Taking a load off things will help you in this season of singleness. As you're healing from past hurt, current letdowns and rejection, pick up your weapon prayer and arm yourself. Seek God on how to release certain situations and individuals from your life. Your time of singleness is the prime time for you to get your life in order and use your time wisely.

Prayer Affirmation

Father, in this time of singleness, please remind us that we are everything with you. Free us from all past hurts and disappointments. Lord, please do an inside job and touch the heart at the very root of the situation. Lord, you said that we can cast all of our cares on you. We're casting every hurt, every sleepless night that was filled with tears on you, Restore those lost moments spent on reliving the past. Wrap your loving arms around us and show us that it is you, Lord, who is our keeper. Amen.

Self-Check

1. How do we fix life's problems?

   _____
   _____
   _____
   _____
   _____

2. How do we handle the toughest situations?

   _____
   _____
   _____
   _____
   _____

3. How do we hang on in the midst of the hardest times?

   _____
   _____
   _____
   _____
   _____

God's Unconditional Love

Over the years, we've heard that no matter what we do, God still loves us. Even in our time of singleness, we must learn to love the one who first loved us. Being single isn't a curse; in fact, this is a prime time for you to strengthen your relationship with Christ. God loves us, in spite of how we feel. Man may throw you away the very moment things go wrong, but we have someone who loves us despite our ways. We serve a mighty God who will never leave or forsake us.

> For the Lord God is a sun and shield;
> The Lord bestows grace and favor and honor;
> No good thing will He withhold from those who walk uprightly.
> Psalms 84:11 AMP

Most of us desire someone to love and cherish us, flaws and all. Singleness is God's gift. Singleness should not be viewed as a problem, and marriage should not be viewed as a right. In His wisdom and love, God grants either as a gift.

Singleness, as a gift? Are you kidding me?! I was shocked and offended the first time my eyes rolled over those words. We may experience loneliness, but if you want to make the most of singleness, here are a few practical points I learned in my own season of waiting.

Embrace your Freedom!

But I want you to be free from concern. The unmarried man is concerned about the things of the Lord, how he may please the Lord; but the married man is concerned about worldly things, how he may please his wife, and *his interests* are divided. The unmarried woman or the virgin is concerned about the matters of the Lord, how to be holy *and* set apart both in body and in spirit; but a married woman is concerned about worldly things, how she may please her husband.
1 Corinthians 7:32-34 AMP

Find and fall in unconditional love with Jesus First!

Jesus is the void filler. God is the mender and healer of the broken heart. He knows all and sees all. He covers us in His blood and we are then forgiven. In whatever season of waiting God may have you in, choose to bloom where you're planted. Embrace the life God has called you to, whether single or married. Trust that both callings are precious gifts of grace, both with painful and overwhelming hardships. Happiness is not found through finding a soul mate, but through finding satisfaction in a loving Savior who has called you His own and made you a daughter of the King.

Be risky

Don't let fear paralyze you and keep you from moving forward in life. God knows exactly what we need and at the appointed time, He will lead us to the one He has for us.
No matter where we are, God will lead us down the path that He would have for us to go.

Sex can wait!

Sex is everywhere. Society paints a picture of it in many commercials, movies and television shows. Society tells us that we can't live without it and that it's completely natural. Sadly, our youth are falling for this trap and are losing their innocence at an alarming rate. God promises to supply all of our need and be our joy and satisfaction. Waiting until God sends your mate is not only an honor for your future spouse, but it is also a way we honor God.

Prayer Affirmation

Father, I come to you fully aware of my need of you. My desire is to seek a stronger relationship with you. You loved me first in spite of it all; you've never left nor forsaken me. Even when I didn't deserve your love, you stood up for me. Father, give me strength to endure all that may come my way. Amen.

Self-Check

What areas of your life do you feel God is molding you in?

_____
_____
_____
_____
_____
_____
_____
_____
_____
_____
_____
_____
_____
_____
_____
_____
_____
_____
_____
_____

Self-Discovery

"Knowing yourself is the beginning of all wisdom."
— Aristotle

Time and time again, we ask, "What is my purpose? What is it that I should be doing?" According to Merriam-Webster Dictionary, self-discovery is *the act or process of achieving self-knowledge.* During your season of singleness, take the time to identify who you are in God, who you are and what you're called to do. This is a never-ending cycle; we're growing and evolving into a new person daily. Our goal should be to find out who we are before we even think about loving someone else.

Self-discovery is a time for us to dig deep into our past and find our purpose. Realize your beliefs and live by them. For years, I waddled in the shadows of my father, unsure of what I was created for. Oftentimes, I compared my situation to the story of David when he was anointed as king. I felt like the anointing, the oil and the hand of God had passed me by. For so long, I really didn't know who I was. I struggled with lack of self-confidence and low self-esteem. For years, I felt that maybe I was just meant to work in the background. Now, I am learning and developing into the individual that God is calling me to be.

Prayer Affirmation

Lord, I thank you for your unfailing love. I thank you for choosing me as your child. Continue to show me who I am in you. Wipe away all confusion so I will stand confidently on what your Word says about me. Your Word declares that I am a royal priesthood; I have been chosen for such a time as this. Help me to see you when I look at myself. Lord, open my eyes and ears so I will hear you ever so clearly. When others speak negatively against what you've called me to be, equip me with the discernment to see through it all. When you made me, you made me in your image and in your likeness. If there be anything in me that shouldn't be, please remove it. Wipe away everything that reminds me of my past. Lord, I trust and believe that you're going to do exactly what you said. In Jesus' name, amen.

Questions for your Self-Discovery

1. Why are you here?
2. What would you like to learn?
3. What brings you joy?
4. What are you most afraid of?
5. What is one step you can take today to move closer to your ideal life?

Faith over Fear

Faith is the complete trust or confidence in someone or something.
(Merriam-Webster Dictionary)

This is a declaration that I've had to recite time and time again. Whenever there's something I desire to do, fear sets in before I can even fully embrace the new task. I am very active in ministry. Oftentimes, I'll have a vision; although I am prayerful in everything, when the rubber meets the road, I battle the fear of being unsuccessful.

Have you ever placed your complete faith and trust in an individual and felt as if you couldn't get out of a situation? How do I know that this is a moment of fear masked by reassurance and other feelings? When things don't add up, you're unsure and uneasy about a situation while fighting it.

Even in relationships, we want the best. We want to experience real love outside of our immediate family. We befriend individuals and even seek companionship. Ultimately, we become so consumed by other parties and their fanfare that we lose ourselves. Yes, ladies I've been there. Sometimes it is fear that keeps us linked to individuals; it's the fear that we cannot regain our strength. It's fear that keeps us in that sunken place. I come to you with confidence to let you know that you can escape the very place of pain. Firstly, seek God if you're unsure that you're stuck in a relationship that's not fruitful. Accept the warning signs that you may have noticed. Don't ignore the signs. A lot of times we feel that we can wait out the red flags of a relationship when that is really pulling on us and stretching us thin. I've known friends and associates to be stuck in relationships and marriages with someone they knew weren't "the one" but because they allowed the fear of what would become of them trap them they settled. Sis you do not have to settle. Seek God, ask him to show you if that individual is for you. Once your intuition gives you the answer you've been seeking please do not pull back in hopes that things will change for the better.

Prayer Affirmation
We know that now faith is the substance of things hoped for, the evidence of things not seen. Through faith, we understand that the worlds were framed by the word of God. Lord, when fear and uncertainty come, send your ministering angels to cover me. Walk beside me, help me to be strong. Through every trial and storm, stretch my faith. I ask you these things in your son Jesus' name, amen.

Romans 5:1, 14:23; Galatians 2:20, 1 Peter 1:6-9

Self-Check

Identify your fight. Whenever we prepare for battle we notice things spiritually and naturally. You must now identify the sources of where your problems stem from. What is it that you are hearing? In what ways will you use the Word of God to combat the situation at hand?

Comfortable with Yourself

The courage to be is the courage to accept oneself, in spite of being unacceptable.
— Paul Tillich

Paul Tillich makes it plain to us. The courage that we need is the courage to accept ourselves even when others do not accept us. To be content is to accept who you are even when others don't. There was a time in my life when I was uncomfortable with myself and my overall appearance. Being uncomfortable with who God had created us to be causes us to doubt ourselves and affects our self-esteem. Growing up, my weight has been on both the plus and the negative sides. I've struggled with confidence and self-esteem. You may look at your reflection in the mirror and grow uncomfortable with what you currently see. You may be a victim of constant jokes or comments.

"Sticks and stones may break my bones, but words may never hurt me."

You have to declare, decree and believe the very words that you speak. Ways that you can become comfortable with yourself are:

- Through proper self-care
- Doing things that makes you happy
- Learning to love your physical flaws
- Embracing your unique personality

- Learning how to be alone

Apply these steps to your life daily and watch things turn around for you.

Prayer Affirmation

Lord, help me to be comfortable with who you have created me to be. Help me to be grateful for all that you have placed inside of me. Lord, help me to love my flaws and all, for they are a part of who I am. In my time of preparation and season of really discovering who I am, Lord help me to love me and to recognize the greatness within. When things come to discourage me, give me the understanding and the strength to overcome it. Help me to see your hand moving in my life. Help me to understand why I was created and to fully accept who I am in you, in Jesus' name, amen.

Self-Check

How much do you worry about what others think?

Trust in the Lord: I Shall Remain Confident

I remain confident of this: I will see the goodness of the Lord in the land of the living.
--Psalms 27:13

Scripture gives us power to remain confident in the Lord. It reminds us that if we remain confident and faithful, we will see the goodness of the Lord. We will be strengthened and empowered to win. We must stand on the very words and promises of God. We fuel our confidence by reciting the word daily. We've learned throughout the years that the Word will not return to the Lord void.

Being confident and trusting in the Lord are the greatest attributes you'll need, especially in your season of singleness. Standing and believing in what the Word of God says concerning us gives us the strength needed to endure. If we focus on what God have for us, then we would ultimately begin to work in those areas He has called us to.

"But seek ye first the kingdom of God, and his righteousness; and all these things shall be added unto you." (Matthew 6:33 KJV) When we seek first

the Father and all of the things of His kingdom, then everything we desire shall be added. For we know that "He is a rewarder of them that diligently seek Him." (Hebrews 11:6) Even when things look like they're failing, just know that all things are working for your good. Remain confident and stay focused on the things of God, knowing that God is with you.

Prayer Affirmation

And this is the confidence that we have in him, that, if we ask anything according to his will, he heareth us:

1 John 5:14

Father, we come boldly before you, asking you to show us the way. Lord, we remain confident in your Word and what it says concerning our lives. Lord, I ask that you touch my mind and remove everything that is not like you. Help us to be the remnant that yet believes and stands on your Word as our foundation. Lord, we know that you do all things well; in your timing, you will show us the way. Lord, prepare us to be ready for what you have for us. Open our eyes that we may see the goodness of the Lord and the ways you've made for us in the spirit. Lord, help us to not be consumed by the words spoken over my life, but to be consumed with the praise that shall go forth in Jesus' name, amen.

Psalms 118:8-9; Jeremiah 17:7; Micah 7:5-7; Hebrews 4:16

1. When do you replace your faith in God with worry?

2. Have you ever been betrayed by a close family member?

3. If we have confidence in God and we solely depend on him, why do we worry and fret over things that he can handle?

A Blessing and a Curse

Behold, I set before you this day a blessing and a curse; A blessing if ye obey the commandments of the Lord your God, which I command you this day. And a curse if ye will not obey the commandments of the Lord your God, but turn aside out of the way which I command you this day, to go after other gods, which ye have not known.

—Deuteronomy 11:26-28

A blessing is God's favor, protection and approval. It is our duty to protect the gift and promises of God. How do we do this? By holding on to God's Word and protecting it with our very lives.

Behold, I set before you a blessing and a curse. Yes, we are all given blessings in many forms. Yes, God has shown you something. Yes, He's given you a word. We must guard that word and believe that God Himself will, in His timing, reveal the moment these words will manifest. We must learn that not every person genuinely cares about our well-being.

Just like the Secret Service and FBI have case-sensitive information that cannot be shared with friends and loved ones, we must also keep those blessings and visions to ourselves. If we aren't careful, the mission, case or situation can be compromised. We have to analyze the situation and then pray strategically. We must use our discernment to see everyone and every situation at face value. Keep those thoughts to yourself and just pray and watch God work on your behalf.

Prayer Affirmation

Heavenly Father, I know that Your word says that death and life are in the power of the tongue; so Lord, help me to keep my words that I won't curse the blessings that you have spoken over my life. Help me with my unbelief in every area. Touch my heart so I will believe and receive everything you have for me. Lord, I thank you for blessing me and making a way for me even when I don't deserve it. Lord, teach me to be quiet when things aren't looking right, or going as planned. Help me to keep myself while I'm in the waiting room of my blessing and promise. Bind every evil force that would have me to speak ill of my blessings, in Jesus' name we pray. Amen!

Psalms 1:1-3; Philippians 4:19; James 1:17

www.ingramcontent.com/pod-product-compliance
Lightning Source LLC
Chambersburg PA
CBHW050651160426
43194CB00010B/1892